How to sell a house

Step-by-step guide outlines how to sell and buy a house:

1. Get your property valued

- Freehold vs Leasehold properties. The difference between these two terms is If you own the property and the land, you're a freeholder, and if you don't own the land, And own the property that it sits on. you're a leaseholder.
- Freehold properties can be sold.
- Leases can be sold.
- You can sell a leased property. As the leaseholder, you have the right to sell your property at any point during the lease. After the lease period you do not own the property. When the lease ends, ownership returns to the **freeholder**, unless you can extend the lease.
- Leasehold purchases can be more complicated, so you should expect higher conveyancing costs.
- Before you start making plans to buy and sell a house at the same time you need to get a clear idea of how much your current home is worth. So search online to see how much similar properties are selling for. Then get at least three local estate agents to give you their valuations.
- Most estate agents will provide you with a valuation for free. The procedure is considered part and parcel of their services.
- If you're considering selling your home and buying another because you need more space, it could be worth comparing the cost of building an extension, converting the attic,? The costs of selling and costs of buying can be significant (particularly with stamp duty (paid if applicable, Stamp duty Tax is subject to change) that it might even save you money to expand your existing home rather than move
- Perhaps you are thinking about downsizing?
- Depending upon your circumstances, you might be better off renting your home out rather <u>than selling</u>

2. Figure out your finances

If you're asking how to sell and buy a house at the same time, the next step is to get your your finances in order. This means you'll need to work out how much can you afford to spend on your next house and how much equity you have in your current home. It helps you figure out how much money you get to, spend and save. Making a budget can help you balance your income with your savings and expenses. It guides your spending to help you reach your financial goals.

- Before you sell your house, you'll want to get a rough idea of how much it is worth. This will also help you calculate how much money will be left if you have a mortgage to pay off.

- Speak to your lender to check if you will have to pay any early repayment charges for switching your mortgage to another lender or whether it is possible to take it with you to a new property
- If you're planning to move to a more expensive property then you may need to remortgage to a better deal.
- At the early stages, figures will be approximate. You don't know how much you will sell for and you will only get a precise redemption (amount outstanding) figure for your mortgage once you have an agreed completion date when you have exchanged contracts

3. Speak to a mortgage broker

- Banks can only offer you their own products. Whereas brokers have access to a wider range of lenders and can offer more deals. Mortgage brokers shop around to find the right mortgage for you. Mortgage broker can be cheaper than banks as they don't have the same overheads.
- Mortgage brokers will offer advice and guidance throughout the process and will also act as your advocate with the mortgage lenders, making it less stressful and increasing your chances of securing a mortgage.
- Mortgage broker fees will remain the same, between 0.3% to 1% of the mortgage amount. With the broker You'll have access to all the deals available in the market.

- A mortgage broker can help guide you to finding the right solution if you're planning on buying and selling a house at the same time. That may involve remortgaging or porting your mortgage. This involves in transferring your existing mortgage to your new property.

- There are 2 types of mortgages that are common in the UK.
  1. (Capital) Repayment Mortgage and
  2. Interest Only

- An interest-only mortgage offers lower monthly payments, but you must pay off the loan in full at the end of the loan term, and they tend to cost more overall.

- While the repayment mortgages may be more expensive each month, they allow you to pay off your mortgage in full and generally cost less over the course of the loan.

- Fixed rate mortgages. With a fixed rate mortgage, you will pay a set rate of interest for a certain number of years. ...

- With an (Standard variable rate).SVR mortgage, your mortgage payments could change each month, going up or down depending on the rate. Mortgage rates are often linked to **the national interest rate**

- I suppose if you can afford it. It works out cheaper in the long term to go for the (Capital) Repayment Mortgage with fixed rate because then you will know what you will be paying out for your mortgage each month.

- The mortgage broker will ask you about your Earning, Wage Slips, Savings and where the money came from?

The documents required for a full mortgage application.

You will usually be asked to provide:

- Photo ID
- Evidence of income (3-6 month's payslips for employed borrowers, accounts or SA302s for self-employed mortgages)
- Three years' address history
- Last three months' bank statements
- Evidence of existing credit and other outgoings
- Details of the property you want to buy (if you already have somewhere in mind)

it's best if your advisor has it all the above for your mortgage application.

Dear Sir/Madam,

Your Ref: A114280002/DLB/SB/Ramsden

Re: Your Client: Ian Ramsden

Property: 11 Hungdington Street, Nottingham, NG9 1NR

Further to your request for my Earnings, Savings, Wages slips. And where my money came from?

I confirm I earn 30k per annum. Please see letter from my employer. And my 6 months wage slips as evidence of income.

Please see my bank statements for last 6 months which show my savings. And also a letter from my brother to show where my money came from? Stocks and share certificates that I sold for my house deposit.

Please do not hesitate to contact me. If you require any further information.

Yours faithfully

Mr Ian Ramsden

Dear Sir/Madam,

Your Ref: A114280002/DLB/SB/Kahn

<u>Re: Your Client: Shelia Ramsden</u>

<u>Property: 11 Hundington Street, Lenton, Nottingham NG7 2WB</u>

I confirm I am providing a gift to my mother in relation to her purchase of the above mentioned property. Please see below information as requested:

1. My full names and address.

    a)
    Ian Ramsden
    11 Hundington Street
    Lenton
    Nottingham
    NG7 2WB

2. My relationship to your client:
    a) My Sister

3. The total amount of the gift and to provide a copy of the bank statements showing the same.

    a) £100,000. Please see bank statements attached.

4. That the gift is non-repayable.

    a) I confirm the gift is non-repayable.

5. That no bankruptcy proceedings are taking place against you.

    a) I confirm no bankruptcy proceedings are taking place against me.

6. That you are not to take up residency at the property or claim any interest.

    a) I confirm I will not take up residency at the property or claim any interest.

7. Copies of your identification in the form of a passport or driving licence.

    a) Please see attached copy of my passport.

Please do not hesitate to contact me. If you require any further information.

Yours faithfully

Mr I Ramsden

4. Choose an estate agent to sell your house

- You normally have 3 options for selling your house. You can sell your home yourself, use a local estate agent or an online estate agent
- If you use a local estate agent, you will need to research which one to choose.
- You will need to agree a fee with the estate agent: aim for 1% plus VAT for sole agent.
- Online estate agents are a cheaper option when selling a house. But you have to deal with them by phone or online.
- Make sure the estate agent has experience of selling property like yours by checking in their shop window, on their website or the property portals. Get a feel for the firm. Look at the properties that the agent sells on Zoopla and Rightmove.
- Valuations aren't always accurate
- Agents commission could be negotiable
- When it comes time to appointing an estate agent, read your contract. Always see what you are being charged to sell your property?
- Some estate agents have been reported putting pressure on people to use their mortgage service, saying they will get preferential treatment By all means, get a quote from the estate agent's mortgage adviser before shopping around, but bear that in mind.
- Agents don't normally tell you what time scale the buyer wants to work by? For example the buyer may be Looking to complete in 20 weeks time. And always get agents to specify the TIME SCALE on the sales memorandum
- A memorandum of sale acts as written evidence that an offer has been accepted, as well as recording the amount of money that will be paid. It is a contract but it's not legally binding.

5. Get an Energy Performance Certificate

It has become law that you have to have a valid EPC. Which lasts for 10 years. If not you will need to get one. It works out cheaper to get your EPC done independently. You can do this by finding local Energy assessors in your area. Getting the ECP through Estate Agents normally works out more expensive.

- An energy performance certificate (EPC) is a document which ranks properties in terms of energy efficiency. Homeowners need to provide an EPC to potential buyers when they sell their home
- You have to have at least applied for an Energy Performance Certificate before you put your home on the market –

6. Decide to sell your home

- You have to decide. what price to put your house on for?
- Do your research and get to know the local market by seeing online how much properties are selling for on the street or local area?
- Get at least 3 estate agents to do valuations, but don't necessarily go for the highest.
- Remember buyers will probably try to negotiate a discount, between 5% to 10%
- Prepare your home for sale

- Tidy up, get rid of excess clutter; give it a fresh light coloured paint;; keep it clean

7. Hire a conveyancing solicitor

- You need to choose a conveyancing solicitor to handle the legal work involved in selling a property.
- To ensure the sale progresses, you should decide which firm you want to use before you agree to the sale of your house. You can obviously only formally instruct after you have agreed an offer
- Get an overview of how much conveyancing fees cost

Dear Sir/Madam,

I am selling a Freehold property.
With approx. value of £255k.

How much will your conveyancing fees be?

Regards

Ian Ramsden

8. Fill out the relevant questionnaires

- You will have a variety of forms, questionnaires and documents to give the buyer all the information about the property, and about the sale.

Good morning

The buyer's solicitor has confirmed the price reduction and issued us with an amended Transfer Deed. They have also sent us some additional enquiries. Please can you provide your written replies to the following, using the same numbering for ease of reference;

1. Please confirm if there is an alarm at the Property. Please confirm all details and that the maintenance contracts etc. will be provided.

2. Please confirm if the Seller has experienced any damp at the Property.

3. Please provide FENSA documentation or building regulations where windows have been replaced.

4. Please supply any warranties or guarantees that the Seller has the benefit of and confirm that they will be assigned to the buyer on completion.

5. Please confirm whether any of the covenants contained within the title have been breached. (copy of title documents attached to assist you)

6. Please confirm if the Property has ever flooded.

7. Please provide a water authority bill and council tax invoice.

8. Please provide a copy of the current insurance policy and schedule.

9. Please provide all plans, electrical and gas certificates, planning and building regulations and completion certificates.

10. Please confirm when the Property was original constructed.

11. Please supply details of the last central heating service and any maintenance contract in place.

12. Please see attached extract from the local authority search and please supply copies of all planning permissions, (extract to follow). - (we have chased this as not yet received)

13. Please supply any indemnity insurance policies in place.

14. Please confirm whether the right of way coloured blue on the Transfer dated 21 May 1980 is in fact used by the council or number 9 Hungerton Street to access their property.

15. Please confirm whether the Seller has been asked to contribute towards the cost of maintenance of the pathway to the rear.

16. Please provide the title to the pathway to the rear. (we have answered this question)

17. Please confirm that all structures have been maintained as party walls and whether there has been any request for contributions towards the adjacent properties for expenses.

18. Please confirm whether any alterations have been carried out at the Property requiring the council's consent.

19. Our client has received a survey to confirm that there is significant damp at the property and this will cost around £6,000 to remedy. Accordingly, we understand that the purchase price is to be reduced accordingly, please confirm. - (please confirm if this is included in the price reduction to £245,000.00.

20. Please provide us with the planning permission in respect of the extension to the rear of the property, together with the building control completion certificate and any warranties available.

We look forward to hearing from you with replies to these enquiries.

Kind regards
Jo Frazer
Conveyancer — Branch Partner

Dear Jo,

Further to the buyers questions, Email dated 13th September 2022.

1) There is no alarm at the property! We have confirmed this in the original paper work!
2) There is no visible damp in the property.
3) There are no FENSA certificates for the windows as these were replaced along time ago. Not available.
4) Not available
5) Not /available
6) When the water mains burst the cellar had water in it. I wound say the water was not excessive but a little bit of water in the cellar.
7) Ok this can be provided.
8) This is not available as our father has now died.
9) Not available
10) We don't know when the property was constructed. All we know is our parents lived here for about 50 years!
11) We have a domestic and general plan to repair the boiler and heating. This will not be passed on to the buyers! As it is not part of the sale contract. They have to take out their own if they wish to.
12) Planning permission was attached.
13) No indemnity policies available.
14) Number 9 have no access from our garden. Number 9 is accessed from the passageway at the back.
15) We have never ever been asked to contribute towards the pathway at the back of the house. There is a solid wall there with fencing on top! We don't even have access to that pathway from our garden.
16) Not available.
17) None
18) Extension to the rear required planning and planning was granted by the council.
19) Yes, this is included in the price! Your client is aware this has been included!
Your client\lender instructed 2 surveyors. The first surveyor was a chartered surveyor who checked for damp, structure of the house, electrics-lighting and everything indoors and outdoors too. And 2nd surveyor checked the woodworks in the whole of the property and damp in the property. Also, your client has inspected the property twice.
20) Planning permission attached
We have answered these questions as best we can.

Regards

Mr Ian Ramsden junior

Hi Jo,

Re: 11 Hundington Street, Lenton, Nottingham NG7 1HL

Further to your email dated 13th September 2022.

I confirm there were NO internal alterations or any type of works that were carried out on 1st March 2022.

To the above mentioned property.

The works were not carried out.

Regards

Mr I Ramsden

Good morning

Thank you for your email with replies. I have checked through these and it appears that you haven't responded to the following;

- How many properties maintain the rear passageway.
- Is the passageway to the site gated and locked? If so, please confirm the keys will be handed over on completion
- Please confirm the type of heating system at the property
- Please confirm when the hearing system/boiler was installed and provide the compliance certificate if necessary.

We look forward to hearing from you with the above four replies so we can reply to all enquiries.

Kind regards

Jo Frazer
Conveyancer – Branch Partner

Dear Jo,

Further to your email dated 24th March 2023.

I agree to provide the indemnity insurance for the double glazing for the sum of £23. I agree to provide this policy on completion and agree that this can be paid from the proceeds of sale.

1.How many properties maintain the rear passageway.
a) Don't know how many properties maintain the rear passageway. Because we don't use the rear passageway. Appears to be clean and tidy. In over 50 years my late husband never maintained it.

2.Is the passageway to the site gated and locked? If so, please confirm the keys will be handed over on completion

a) It is gated and has got a padlock on the inside. So, nobody can get in from outside. We can provide the current padlock to the new owner.

3. Please confirm the type of heating system at the property

a)The property has got a gas combination boiler central heating system

4. Please confirm when the hearing system/boiler was installed and provide the compliance certificate if necessary.

a)Installed Over 6 years. We don't have a completion certificate. We have got an extended warranty with the manufacture\domestic and general. The manufacture maintains the boiler. We can't provide the warranty to the new buyer.

Kind regards

Ian Ramsden

Good morning

The buyer's solicitor is obtaining indemnity insurance for the lack of planning consent. We don't feel that this is necessary and have informed them to obtain this at their own expense, however, they have asked that as seller you can confirm the following statement of facts in the policy;

1. No application for consent has previously been refused and/or application made to obtain retrospective consent, in respect of the works
2. You are not aware of any adverse features and/or recommendations for remedial action, in respect of the works
3. The local authority has not indicated any intention to investigate or take action in relation to the works The property is a single, stand-alone, private residential dwellinghouse or purpose-built flat, rather than a holiday let and/or property formed from a converted building, a house in multiple occupation, or an additional, self-contained dwelling ancillary to the main dwelling.
4. Cover is only required for alterations previously carried out to the property
5. The works to be covered were completed at least 6 months ago ('works' can include extensions, additions and alterations)

Please can you read through these and agree that they are confirmed.

Kind regards
Jo Frazer

Dear Jo,

Absolutely I agree this indemnity needs to be paid for by the buyers!

1) Initially we applied for a two storey Extension on the house, the council stated they will only give us consent for a single storey Extension! Hence we have a single storey Extension on the house. (the downstairs Wet-room). Just past the kitchen.

2) We are not aware of any remedial features.

3) The property is a semi-detached property. The council had consented to the Extension at the back of the house. They have never said there was anything wrong with it and we haven't noticed anything wrong with it. Our father lived in the property for 50 years and he never complained about anything.

It's just a main home. It was never a holiday home. It was always a family home.

Always been my father's main home. No alterations have been carried out to this property since 2002.

4) There have not been any alterations, except the Extension on the property in 2002.

5) We have not had any works done to the property in the last 6 months! In fact, the last lot of works was the Extension which was completed in 2002. We have not added any recent Extension's except what is already mentioned. We have never knocked out any walls in the home. All the walls are original.

Regards

Mr I Ramsden

9. Requesting a copy of the planning consent and completion certificate for a extension on existing your property from the council. That you are trying to sell. You Will need the above documents before you can sell.

Dear Sir/Madam,

Re: 11 Huntingdon Street Lenton Nottingham NG7 2WB

Ref: 00/06098786/DEX : Single storey rear shower room extension.

I am the owner/vendor of the above-mentioned property.

My buyer's legal team are requesting a copy of the planning consent.
(I have already obtained a copy of the completion certificate).

Could you please let me know, if the copy of the planning consent is still available?
For the above mentioned property.

I look forward to hearing from you.

Yours sincerely

Mr I Ramsden

10. Accept an offer

- You've received an offer – The estate agent is legally required to pass all offers on to you
- Before you accept an offer, take a look at the different types of buyers and how to deal with their offers
- If you are not happy with the offer, you can either reject it outright, wait to see if a better offer comes along, or tell the estate agent to try to negotiate it upwards
- Once you are happy with an offer, you need to formally accept it.
- Remember that accepting an offer is not legally binding, and you can legally change your mind or accept a higher offer later

Dear Amanda,

Re: final offers for 11 Hundington Street, Lenton Nottingham

My final offer for the above property is £245.500. I have £100.000 cash. I am exchanging contracts for my property and completing, within a period of 2 weeks, as advised by my legal team. From the sale I expect to spend 75,000 on this property. Also I have a provisional offer of a mortgage, for £80.000

As advised by my financial consultant. I can change the amount on the provisional mortgage. I will require to have a survey from my lender. I am happy to aim to complete the purchase to suit the seller. Ie if I require less then £80,000 the borrowing can be reduced.

I have chosen the following solicitors:-

Haus Solictors
299 Main Street
Bulring
Nottingham
NG6 3AK

Hope this is all that is required to make a final bid. If any further information is required, please do not hesitate to contact me.

Thank you for your help in dealing with this matter.

Yours Sincerely

Ian Ramsden
07779750076

Dear Heather,

I am writing to let you know that we have a new buyer for the property,
I have accepted offer from Grant & Warner Ltd, offer of £245,000.

New Estate Agents are involved their details are as follows:

King Estate Agents
13/18 Upper Parliament Street Nottingham,
Nottinghamshire NG1 2NR
T 0115 941 1311
E nottingham@king.co.uk

Please proceed with the sale.

If you have any further queries, please do not hesitate to contact me contact me

Yours sincerely

Mr I Ramsden
Mobile: 07535 648 073

11. Arrange survey/Valuation

- Arrange survey/valuation: Sometimes the lender will send their surveyor.
- If you wish to arrange a home valuation, contact local surveyors who are registered with the Royal Institution of Chartered Surveyors. You can discuss your requirements and find out more about fees and availability.
- I normally go for a level 2 home buyers report. The level 2 survey report uses a 'traffic light' ratings system to describe the condition rating of the property's
- Main features (such as glazing, roof, electrics, plumbing and exterior. Reports might find things such as damp, Foundation problems, subsidence or thermal cracks.
- With a level 2 survey you will find out whether the house has got any main problems however you can go for more detailed survey. Depending on what your requirements are:

Sample Email querying a survey report.

Dear Sir/Madam,

Further to the surveyors report. Could you please ask the vendor has he got copies of the following reports? If yes could he please provide us with the following reports?

D4 - External walls Cavity Wall insulation certificate/guarantee
D5 - Windows Double glazing - FENSA certificates/guarantees
D6 - External
Doors FENSA certificates/guarantees
F1 - Electricity NICEIC/NCA test certificates.
F2 - Gas 'Gas Safe' registered engineer's safety test certificate.
F4 - Heating 'Gas Safe' registered engineer's test of the central heating

Following the survey from the surveyor he has picked on the following problems with the property:-

1. Where walls are tile hung, it is not possible to comment specifically on the condition of the
construction beneath. The claddings may conceal distortions, cracks or other defects

There are a number of spalled bricks below the damp proof course, particularly to the left hand
side elevations, which should be replaced to prevent potential penetrating dampness. Condition
Rating 2.

PAGE 18

2. Dampness is present at lower levels to the walls particularly to the understairs external wall and
the kitchen external wall, and further investigation to the whole property is required before exchange of contracts

PAGE 18

3. There is a risk that metal ties built into cavity walls constructed before 1982 will corrode. There are
they have corroded but the need for eventual wall tie replacement
should be anticipated.

4. There is evidence that cavity wall insulation is installed, but the material cannot be determined.
Legal adviser to verify the type of insulation. If foam has been used there have been problems with
this material. In time it can deteriorate, cause damp penetration and/or result in accelerated
corrosion of wall ties (see Section H2)

DAMPNESS TO INTERNAL WALLS
PAGE 19

5. Windows are a mix of anodised aluminium, uPVC and timber framed, which are double glazed to
the front and left hand hand side and single glazed to the rear.
Sealed units are prone to failure causing misting between the glazing. Due to the weather conditions faulty units may not be apparent and future replacement should be anticipated. Legal
adviser to establish if there is a guarantee (see Section H2).
The quality of sealed unit double glazed windows varies and no assurances can be given concerning long term durability.

3

E2 CEILINGS
6. The plasterboard ceilings were found to be level and without any undue
    vibration, when subject to light fingertip pressure. Condition Rating 1.
There is potential for localised hairline cracking to occur along the plasterboard joints as a result of
thermal/moisture movement
PAGE 24

7. The floorboards are loose throughout out the first floor and should be re-
    fixed. Improved support
may be needed in some places. Condition Rating 2.
PAGE 25

8. There is some unevenness to the floor in the entrance hall and you should lift
    the carpets to ensure the floor slab is in sound condition and free from any
    defect. Condition Rating 3 – Further

Investigation

PAGE 25

9. If a recent test certificate, dated within the last 12 months, is not available
    for the installation and any electric appliances, then I recommend they are
    tested (see Sections H2 and I3).
I recommend you obtain a report and quotation from a qualified electrician (for example NICEIC/
ECA Registered) for complete re-wiring/partial re-wiring of the property. Condition Rating 3

PAGE 29

10. Mains gas supply is connected with the meter located in the under stairs
    cupboard.
If a recent test certificate, dated within the last 12 months, is not available for the gas
supply and appliance(s) then I recommend they are tested (see Section H2 and I3).
Condition Rating 3.I recommend mains powered carbon monoxide detectors are fitted as
there are none installed (see Section I3). Condition Rating 3.Arrange for a report and
quotation from a 'Gas Safe' registered engineer for any recommended
work with subsequent test certificate. Condition Rating 3.

PAGE 30

11. I recommend you obtain a report and quotation from a 'Gas Safe' registered
    engineer in respect of
the central heating system. Condition Rating 3

12. The garage is in a poor condition to include damaged asbestos panels which will require removal and replacement taking into account the necessary safety precautions when dealing with asbestos
13. materials, and repairing the lintel over the front door. See section I3. Condition rating 3- further investigation

14. There is significant waterlogging to the front garden and repairs to the drains are required. Condition Rating 3 - further investigation. The tarmac drive is in a poor condition and requires repair or renewal. Condition Rating 3

Being upfront with the vendor about what your survey has shown, including any costs associated with fixing them is a perfectly fair reason for renegotiating on the price.

The above areas are causing concern after the survey with me and I have highlighted the areas that are causing me concern.

The inspection has identified potential problems red flags (**water issues, damp, electrics not up to date, uneven floor and requires lintel above front door**)

I believe is very likely that neither the vendor, or the estate agent would have known about any problems beforehand, and it is entirely reasonable to negotiate a house price after a survey and provide a counter offer if things have changed.

Therefore I am of opinion I get a local builder to price up the essential works. And to re-negotiate price. Could you please talk to the vendor. And ask whether he is willing to re-negotiate the price?

Regards

Shiraz Janjua

Sample Email asking to reduce price from the House Sale

Dear John Smith,

I am writing to make you aware to let the Vendor know. I want to go ahead with the purchase and will be looking to exchange contracts over the next couple of weeks, As advised by My Legal Team. Repairs are clearly needed. However I would ask that either the above items including the damp and drains are addressed, or we agree a reduction in the purchase price of

£XXXX and I'll handle the repair works to the property after I move in. To substantiate information my please see invoices attached for the damp and the drains.

Respectfully could you please let the vendor know. That other buyers will face exactly the same problem!

Could you please ask the vendor. How he wants to proceed?

Yours Sincerely

Shiraz Janjua

12. Notify Estate agents which solicitors firm you will be using:-

Hi Tracy,

I would like to use the following solicitors firm:-

King Solictors
299 Main Street
Bulring
Nottinghamshire
NG6 8ED

0115 955 3444

My solicitors name is Jo Frazer

Regards

I Ramsden

13. Estate agents will generate a sales memorandum. Once a Sale is agreed between the buyer and seller.

What is a Memorandum of Sale?

- A memorandum of sale acts as written evidence that an offer has been accepted, as well as recording the amount of money that will be paid. It is a contract but it's not legally binding. It's a preliminary measure to set out the terms of agreement before parties have to legally commit.

- After an offer has been agreed. If the agents don't generate a sales memo. Then chase them for the sales Memorandum. Sales memorandum confirms the house is subject to contract.

MEMORANDUM OF SALE

Subject to Contract

DATE: 16th June 2023

PROPERTY: 11 Hundington Street, Lenton, Nottingham, NG7 3WB

SELLER:
Ian Ramsden
22 Eden Close
Beeston
Nottingham
NG9 2HL

SELLER'S SOLICITORS:
Ms Frazer
King Solicitors
299 Main Street
Bulring
Nottingham
NG6 8NR
01159 881470
JoFrazer@king-solicitors.co.uk; info@king-solicitors.co.uk

BUYER:
Anna Barack
17 Water Lane
London
SE14 5DD

BUYER'S SOLICITORS:
Ms Jessica Banout

JMW Solicitors
1 Byrom Place
Spinningfields
Manchester
M3 3HG
0161 777 1099
Jessica.Banout@jmw.co.uk

AGREED SALE PRICE: £230,000

GENERAL COMMENTS: Looking for completion in 4 weeks.

- After an offer has been agreed. If the agents don't generate a sales memo. Then chase them for the sales Memorandum. Sales memorandum confirms the house is subject to contract.
- A memorandum of sale acts as written evidence that an offer has been accepted, as well as recording the amount of money that will be paid. It is a contract but it's not legally binding. It's a preliminary measure to set out the terms of agreement before parties have to legally commit.

14. Contact solicitor to proceed with sale

Dear Jo,

Re: 11 Main Street, Lenton, Nottingham NG7 1NR

I am writing to inform you that the previous buyers have fallen
Out of the purchase.

Please see Memorandum of Sales attached above with
New Buyer details.

Please proceed with the sale.

Yours sincerely

Mr I Ramsden

15. Negotiate the draft contract

You and the buyer will have to decide:

- The length of time between exchange and completion (usually 7-28 days after the exchange of contracts)
- What fixtures and fittings will be included – and how much will they pay for them
- Any discounts due to problems flagged up by the survey

Dear Jo,

The King Estate Agents contacted me today, and stated the buyers solicitors are still waiting for the draft contract of sale. From communication I understand it has already been sent out to the buyers solicitors.

Could you please confirm, whether the 'draft contract of sale' has been posted out to the 3rd party's solicitors?

I look forward to hearing from you.

Yours sincerely

Mr I Ramsden

16. Exchange contracts

- When you exchange contracts with the buyer, you become legally committed to selling the property – and they are legally committed to buying it from you
- If you pull out after this without due reason, the buyer's deposit will be returned to them and you may be sued

17. Move out

- You can move out whenever you like, including on the day of completion
- It is less stressful to move out beforehand, if that is possible (if you have somewhere to move to)
- At the time of completion, the property has to be in the condition agreed in the contract including all the fixtures and fittings
- The buyer and estate agent may come round between your moving out and completion to ensure that everything is in place
- Plan your move with writing down everything that needs to be done? When tasks are complete from your Moving House Checklist then tick them off.

- ## Checklist for moving into a new house

- **1. Begin to declutter**

- **2. Take measurements of your new home**

- **3. Organise and schedule movers**
- Three months out from a move is a very reasonable amount of notice to give if you're looking to hire a professional removal company for your relocation.

- **4. Start packing non-essential items**

- **5. Book your annual leave**

- **6. Start planning how to use up opened items**

- **7. Order any essential moving supplies**
- such as packing tape, sturdy moving boxes, sticky labels, permanent markers for writing onto said labels and bubble wrap – and order them in if not.
- top packing tip, invest in clear boxes instead of boxes for regularly used items.
- 'Clear boxes will enable you to locate items quickly, and it will look and feel less overwhelming in the new space when it comes to unpacking.'
- Label boxes for each room ie kitchen bedroom 1 Bedroom 2 garage, Shoes and etc. So you can find the items easier at the new house.
- **8. Make a list of people to notify of your move**
- With just four weeks until you're out of your current property, it's important to put together a list of people/organizations who need to know that you're moving. This might include your workplace, your bank, household service providers
- **9. Start packing more of your items**

- **10. Put together a moving binder**
- Of vital importance in your moving house checklist is arranging all of the relevant documents that moving requires. As such, Ian advises that you should 'definitely keep a binder or digital file of all essential documents – staying organized is a big factor in keeping the stress down.'
- Assemble all relevant paperwork, such as insurance papers, contracts, an inventory if you are renting your current property, and any useful receipts. You never know when you might need them all!
- **11. Label boxes according to your new home**

- **12. Pack kitchen items you don't use regularly**

- **13. Investigate home insurance**
- Take a moment to organize your home insurance policy at this point – speak to your current supplier to see whether you can move your policy over to your new property, or whether you'll need to take out a new one with a different supplier for your area.
- **14. Move items into storage if necessary**

- **15. Pack important items you want to keep an eye on**
- There are many precious items that you'll want to keep track of as you move between homes, to avoid damages, losses, or even the potential for theft. Because of this, pack these with just a week to go, so you know where they are at all times.
- In fact, Sarah even advises, 'Pack important documents, jewellery, and valuable items separately from everything else, and transport them yourself for added security.

- **16. Box up those remaining items**

- **17. Put together a bag of essentials**
- The days after your big move will probably be slightly chaotic. As such, one brilliant tip for your checklist for moving into a new house is to pack a suitcase containing only the key items you'll need in the days after getting settled into your new home.
- 'Pack everyone's pajamas, toothbrushes, bed sheets, blankets, pillows and a couple of outfits, to make the first night and next morning less stressful,'
- **18. Action your change of address**
- Remember that list you jotted down weeks ago as part of your moving house checklist? Now is the time to action it, and notify all relevant parties of your change of address.
- For example, get in touch with your new doctor's office, optometrists, gym, and your new town council.
- **19. Clean your new home**

18. Complete the sale

- Completion is when the property changes ownership, you accept payment, and hand over the keys
- It takes place on a previously agreed date and usually at midday
- On the day of completion, the money is transferred and any deeds for the property are transferred between each side's solicitor
- Your solicitor will register the transfer of ownership with the Land Registry

1. Pay off the mortgage

- The mortgage company will have given you and your conveyancing solicitor a precise redemption figure (outstanding amount) for your mortgage for the day of completion
- Now the buyer has transferred the money to your conveyancing solicitor, they will pay off the mortgage for you

20. Settle up with the conveyancing solicitor and estate agent

- After completion, your conveyancing solicitor will send you an account, covering all their costs and disbursements, as well as the sale price of the house and redemption of the mortgage
- If you are buying and selling at the same time, the conveyancing solicitor can settle up for both transactions at the same time, including paying stamp duty paid if applicable for the house you are buying
- Your conveyancing solicitor will ensure that the change of ownership is registered with the Land Registry

Summary:-

Buying and selling a house at the same time

1. Get your property valued by 3 agents at least.
2. Work out your finances. Before you decide to move.
3. Speak to a mortgage broker. To find out what deals will meet your needs?
4. Get your EPC. Otherwise you can't put your property on the market.
5. Dig out these key documents. Energy performance certificate (EPC) and etc
6. Contract for sale & Transfer deed.
7. Prepare your home for sale. Get rid of the clutter. Tidy up. And paint your house.
8. Find an estate agent & market the property.
9. Choose a conveyancing solicitor.

Step by step process of selling a house

This guide to selling a house begins at the point that you accept an offer on your property. The house selling guide steps will then include:

- Instruct solicitor for your house sell
- House deeds obtained
- Draft contract submitted to buyer's solicitor
- Contract signed by sellers and buyers
- Contracts exchanged, deposit paid and completion date agreed
- On completion buyer pays balance of purchase price to seller's solicitor who hands over the house deeds and the keys are released to the buyer

What is the homebuying process step by step?

The step-by-step guide to buying a house begins as soon as you've had an offer accepted on a property. The next steps are:

- Instruct solicitor (look at reviews online or ask family and friends go by recommendation)
- Make mortgage application: Submitting bank statements for mortgage applications is typically a necessary part of the underwriting process when getting approved for a loan. Lenders want to look at it to verify your employment, assets, income, and monthly debt obligations that were outlined in your mortgage loan application
- Arrange survey/valuation: Normally Arranged via Estate Agents

- Searches carried out and enquiries raised
- Draft contract received and information regarding the property checked
- Contract signed by sellers and buyers
- Contracts exchanged, deposit paid and completion date agreed
- On completion buyer pays balance of purchase price to seller's solicitor who hands over the house deeds and the keys are released to the buyer
- Stamp duty paid if applicable and the land registry is notified of the new owners' details.

Real Estate in the UK

The property purchase process in the UK?

There are no restrictions on foreign ownership. At present. The law does change from time to time.

Buying property

Buying property in UK can be summarized in 3 stages: the search and offer, conveyancing and the final touches.

1. Find a suitable property and make an offer, usually through your real estate agent.

2. After your offer has been accepted you may wish to arrange for a survey. A survey is strongly advised for early detection of potential problems carried out by charted surveyor. I am of the opinion best to go for a level 2 survey so the surveyvor can pick up any problems with the house. Generally there are two kinds of survey:

- a building survey
- a homebuyer´s report, which will be cheaper

The types of property investment you could go for include:

- Buy-to-let
- Property development
- Buying a new build to sell on
- Investing in property
- Real estate investment trusts and other property investment funds

If you fancy yourself as a property developer, when you buy a property to refurbish or renovate and sell on, you need to know the risks as well as the potential rewards.

What Is a Real Estate Investment Trust (REIT)?

A real estate investment trust (REIT) is a company that owns, operates, or finances income-generating real estate.

Modelled after mutual funds, REITs pool the capital of numerous investors. This makes it possible for individual investors to earn dividends from real estate investments—without having to buy, manage, or finance any properties themselves.

Property funds are investments in commercial property, for example, offices, factories, warehouses and retail space. Customers make lump-sum investments, which are pooled together and used to purchase a range of assets. As with all investments, property funds do carry a risk. Therefore property funds are risky. The risk is a necessary part of the deal when seeking to make a profit. The value of the buildings and the amount of rental income they can generate can go down as well us up in commercial property.

Selling a property

A Home Information Pack (HIP) must now be provided before properties in England. The pack must contain:

- An energy Performance Certificate
- A sale statement
- A copy of the title documents for the property
- Local Authority and drainage searches
- An index

If the property is leasehold or commonhold, then the pack must also include the following:

- A copy of the lease
- Building insurance policy
- Contact details for the landlord or management and any legal details
- Regulations that apply
- Recent service charge receipts and accounts

law is complex and is changing rapidly. Obtain legal advice on your own specific circumstances and check whether any relevant rules have changed.

Printed in Great Britain
by Amazon

40751194R00020